YEAR OF THE INVERTED STAR

Matthew Kosinski is a poet, socialist and occultist from Philadelphia. Find more of his work at linktr.ee/velmatrout.

Also by Matthew Kosinski

Your Human Shape	(Broken Sleep Books, 2021)
Alone in the White Marble City	(New Delta Review, 2020)

CONTENTS

For Nico and for others.

ISBN: 978-1-917617-61-1

Cover designed by Aaron Kent

Cover image: © Patrick P. Palej/ Adobe Stock

Broken Sleep Books Ltd
PO BOX 102
Llandysul
SA44 9BG

Year of the Inverted Star

Matthew Kosinski

Broken Sleep Books

Conception Dream

it all, like an old god, rises stinking

from the fluids; there is no other way to come
into being.

(a)

shit — life spreads

through channels, canals,

mouth :: mouth

contaminant. interpenetrant.
but it's not anti-social to say so: life

as a principle • as a matter of principle
punctures the membranes.

seep and bleed
seep and bleed
seep and bleed
seep and bleed
seep and bleed
seep and bleed

— Don Giovanni,

Søren, obscure, claps for you, as a principle,
soak the cast through. break the arms of the church. take up trepanation.
find ways to get inside one another, as a principle.

t h e
c e l l | admits
t h e
v i r u s

accepts
the | his
ash | rescue
breath

t h e
animal

———

a s s e m b l e s
i t s e l f
a c c o r d i n g
t o
a set
o f
instructions

two heterosexuals in love do the most boring thing possible.

//   its dirt lungs thicken with oxygen.

still, it's a qualitative change, a new
groove ground in the quantum potential.

consciousness wells up like a tear
collecting on the rim of its vessel.

•

life, with a covert motion, carves
a sluice to route the overflow.

slosh
lash & &
schlick

— the sound of an eyeball escaping its socket.

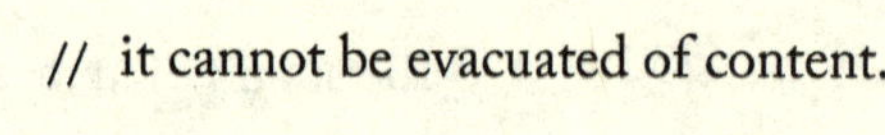

// it cannot be evacuated of content.

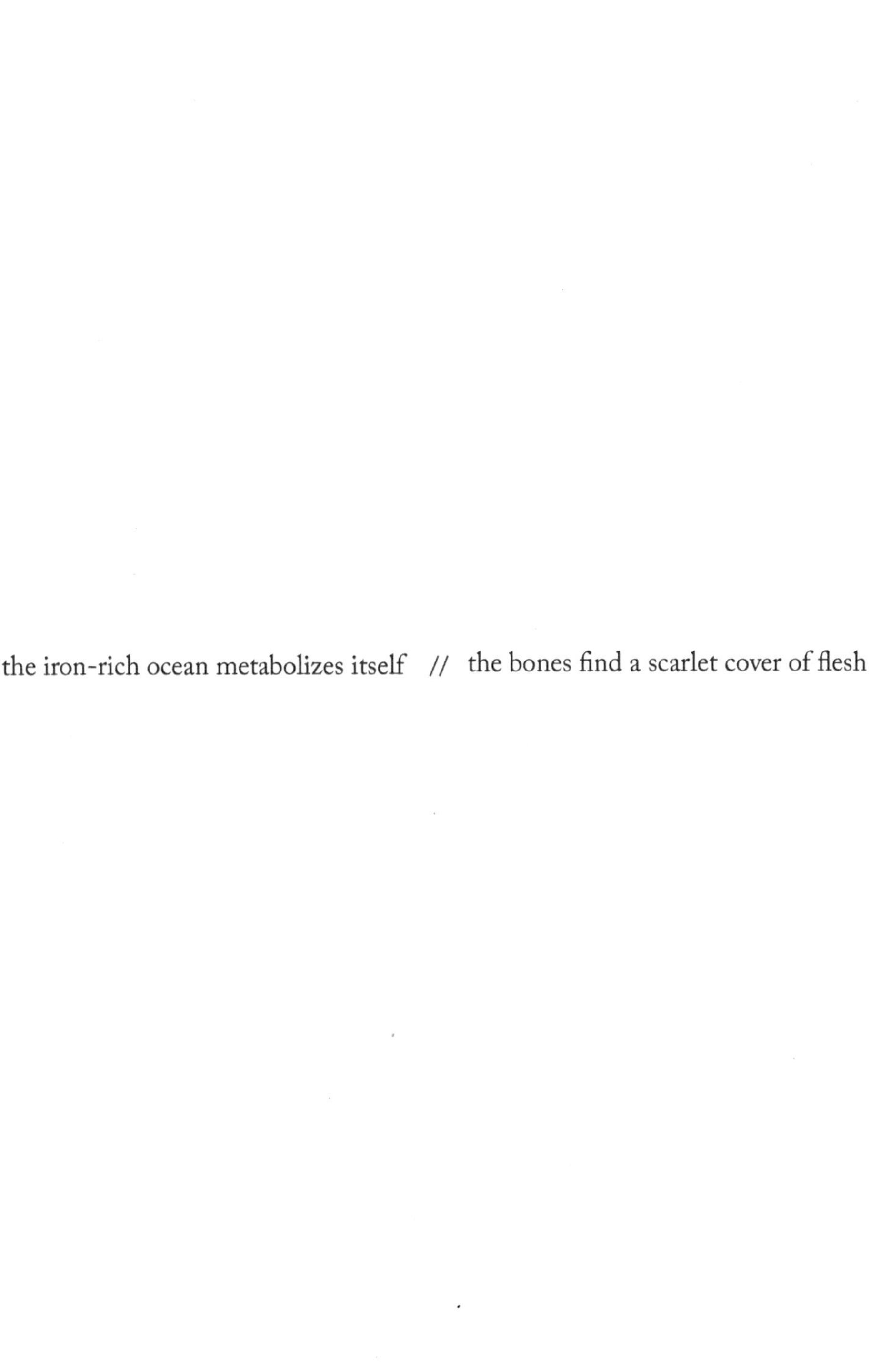

the iron-rich ocean metabolizes itself // the bones find a scarlet cover of flesh

magnetically,
which is to say,
fundamentally.

two strangers are Don Giovanni to one another.

they unfold in time,
which is to say,
like music; like water

they erode the coasts on a long enough line.

how liquid? it all is. how easily:
life takes your heart | the heart stands in for the whole | the inert cosmos twinkles with a generative foam | something wholly heretofore unknown
crawls out of a cavern in the declarative mode.

(as a principle.)

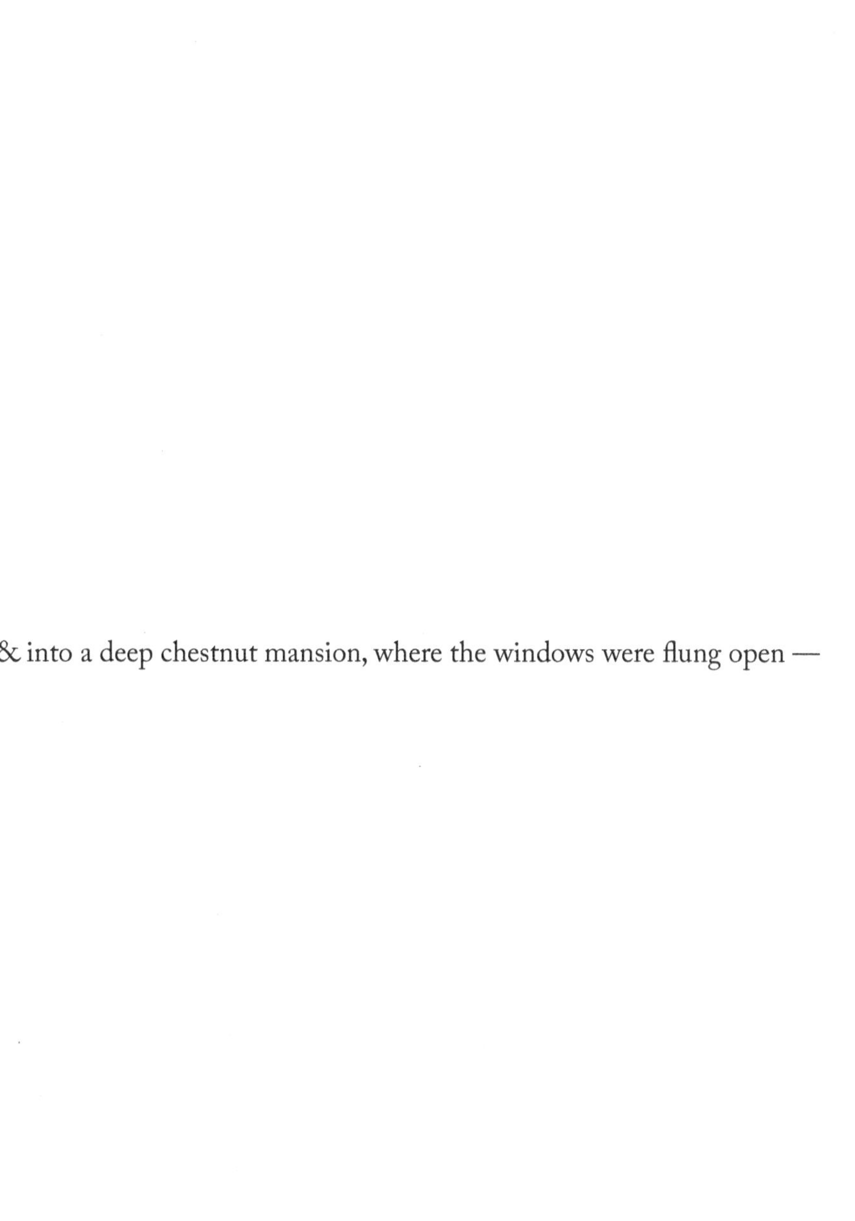

& into a deep chestnut mansion, where the windows were flung open —

life boils in the tissue of a comely finger,
shakes its little omens from its hair

(we get into each other)

like seeds.

(my trypophile.)
porousness is
our imperative

at the
particulate
level: a mystic
looking at
the marsh
and thinking,

yes, this'll do.

,XXXXXX XXXXXX X XX XXXXXX XXX XX XXXXX XXXX
XXXX XXX XXXX XXXXX XXXXXX XXX XXXXXX

(XXXXX XXXX XXXX XXX XX)

.XXXXX XXXX

(.XXXXXXXXXX XX)
XX XXXXXXXXXX
XXXXXXXXXX XXX

XXX XX
XXXXXXXXXXX
XXXXXXX X:XXXXX
XX XXXXXXX
XXXXX XXX
,XXXXXXXX XXX

.XX XX'XXXXX ,XXXX

Three Years

1. My Christ Year

I renounce the pleasurable
droplets condensed on the manuscript

like gooseflesh,
like strawberry
skin.

Gods go hunting for this stuff,
you know.
Cloaks
rippling
from
their
eye-
walls.

Skinny beautiful
arms pull
the mortals apart.

Xxx xx xxxxxxx xxx xxxx xxxxx
xxx xxxxx
Xxxxx
xxxxxxxx
xxxx
xxxxx
xxx
xxxxx

[And the cheap gem in the lovers' heart
flashes me through the centuries]

There are so many interesting things to think about.

Why would I ever think about sex?

When the carcasses |
pile |
up | giant crosses sleeping
at | in the deep landscape?
the | We have them like weather.
bases of | they come to pass, they fade
away.

America thrills to a destiny

Xxxx xxx xxxxxxxx
xxxx
xx
xx
xxx
xxxxx xx

a rotten quiet eating through
the bones of the murderous
restaurant

Oc-
culted,
un-
cursed
a dis-
cor-
dant
techne

ripens like the wheatcrop.

I’ve never used a metaphor | not once in my life.

When I said,

it was real.

xxx

xxxxx

xxxx

xxxxxxxx

xxxxX

xxxxx xxx

xxxxx xxxx xxx xxxxxxx xx xxX

"I will become an empty crystal goblet refracting the light,"

xxxxx xxxx xxx xxxxxxx xx xxX

xxxxx xxx

xxxxX

xxxxxxxx

xxxx

xxxxx

xxx

xxxxx

Three Years

2. My Katsuragi Year

I've denied it, my cup, my golden
cup bearing a hot rich wine.

There are so many interesting thoughts worth having:

red water laps at the roots of the high-rise,
thin lips hunt through the dark and the alarum,
fingers spill like milk all over the piano keys.

Amassing, as I go, a collection of controversial talismans
in service of saying something troublingly Jungian.

Every abstract shape in the terrain has innervated and enflamed.
Why wouldn't it all be sex?

But the raw anomie of the hospital scene calls for a counterpoint:

---

a noble crime, a special crown
I place upon your head as I push you through the elevator doors.

Aleph, shekhinah, the archetype, he said, is simply the image
a mind makes to make sense of its instincts.

The grinning freak descending from our blown-open heaven?
That's it.

Three Years

3. Year of the Inverted Star

in which the self is understood
to be a brilliant moon, involute and still,
above a thirsting void.

The hells of other people thread the ink-dark fog
like fulgurite veins in the shoreline,
like a bitcrushed guitar swathed in string.

We invent intricate solipsisms to carry on with it.

But you are handsomely futured;
Your milky hair chimes with clotted ice;

---

you wear the vernix caseosa in the expanded field.
salt and particular. The cloudcover lifts.

My philosophy is simple now. What is needed
to accommodate you is an idea that never doubles back on itself,
the shape of a thought of affection:

———————————————

Desire, everted, like a shark's stomach, exposed to air.

Some of Them Barked Like Dogs

Sister Jeanne des Anges
Loudun, 1634

I. Her Forehead

A shape is being taken. That which lies behind
advances. To the fore, to those forbearing
in the noplace of screaming relics, the constant unconsummated
ascension: the fleshly world arrives with its tentacles to the sanctuary.
Its tentacles of total comprehension. The act is the awareness, and the awareness
inheres to the underside of the action. The gesture, contratemplative,
outstretched, and not up-. Toward, and not away,
the worldly flesh. The forspoken ground returns in a rush like a ridden horse,
panting. Soil in my mouth from its long long long long legs.
Long in the direction of the horizon. Outward, not higher.
Expansive as distinct from finer. Vision widens from a pinpoint,
compounds like an eye. And the body, deaccessioned, becomes a body entirely

of appendages:

arms for shins and
arms for thighs and
arms for a liver and
arms for lungs and
arms for a heart and
arms for arms and
arms for a neck and
arms for a brain.

Every wrist begins with a hand.

At Compline the others grow inwardly into the caramel cores of
candies in their shut cells. At the edge of the waking day
we waken further to the Forest of Things. Creaturehood, recovered
in the weedy excess of material. We no longer keep the canonical hours.
Crawling on a thousand palms, inlaid, immanent, knowing by touch
the olivine deposits, the decorative cinnabars, the many hard fruits of phenomena.
In the kingdom of light it all cleaves to the surface. A windless avenue of exteriors.
We otherwise, infixed, tellurian: star-slyme spatters our night's deep features.
Rather unlike the rains it wells up from the interior. Come
Matins the lower parts of the skies brighten.
We look up from the changes and discover more changes.
Some of us swear and blaspheme. Some of us bark like dogs.

II. The Last Rib of Her Right Side

The pope decamped from Avignon some centuries ago.
The cardinal nestles in our outskirts. His red eminence
swells through the woods in the evenings.

We had been hung up on the Idea
like a gallows. While they assiduously emptied the earth
of its organs and sweetmeats. Still the convent

could not shut it out. The unbuckled belt
of touching. The hawthorn branch the handsome priest
passed through the gates. The stench of rot

soaked the air, evidence of an actual
and unattractive somewhere. A shape
is being taken to the breast and nursed, emerging in space.

• a point

—— a line

> an angle

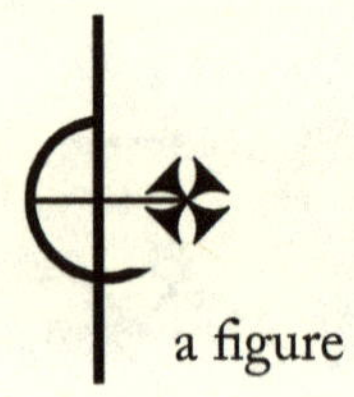
a figure

Following our senses out of the dark night
we came to the last unblasted grove,
the necrotizing wound from which the liquor puris flows.

And the flocks of kings'
ministers cried *ius novissimum* and *salve regina.*
Truth is the gorgeous preacher locked in the iron shoes

was not a catalyst, but an excuse. We chose
to burn our bones on the braken altar. We grew beards of copper,
we grew beards of silver, and of coal. We cut the slits below our hearts,

long as pins, not emptying, but expressing
what condenses when the substance sublates the spirit.
When the exorcists arrive from the central office

I let them lead me to the stage in chains. So I might vomit
strange objects for the people: maggots and needles,
toads of clay. So I might engage in light impact play:

slap their fathers, pull their mothers' unwashed hair. The crowd roars
when we wrestle the presbyters to the floor.
The pope will flee again, yes. This time, even from Rome.

III. The Base of Her Stomach

A church owl tears the stitches from the night. The firmament's fabrics
flap like several wings, making a virtue of presence.
I will not succumb to a jizzy god. I will not
develop the spermy wet brain of the cloisters. A pregnant pure mind, the carcass
withers.
The devils in the meanwhile recline in dishabille.
They cavort in fields of French roses. They kiss our assholes on the sabbath.

People say this: Possession is a kind of penetration. The townsfolk and the scholars both. The foreign soul pierces the familiar body, deposits a corrupting filth. Taste of ash, a taste for choking. Undiluted lemon and overripe shallot. In from the outside. But the doctrines have got it all backward: It's how we get out from the in-. It's there in the name, Old French *possesser*. The receptive end, extension and surrounding. A shape is being, taken. Assumed. The hierarchs as you well know stripped our vessels from us long ago, made of us all a temple below the throat. Thus we pushed our wholeselves monklike into our skulls, into the quiet astral rooms in contemplation, where we begged to go up one day in a smoke, as if from a censer, and luxuriate the holy nose. But possession affords another logic, an enveloping, a sensuous hole. Through which one could climb back down and out into the warm urgent pits of the world. *The crowd roared when we wrestled the presbyters* yes because we wrapped their stately rites in bangles. We made the speech of prayer twist to moans.

Consobrinus Universalis

universal cousin the universal cousin the universal cousin the universal cousin the universa
n the universal cousin the universal cousin the universal cousin the universal cousin the
ersal cousin the universal cousin the universal cousin the universal cousin the universa
n the universal cousin the universal cousin the universal cousin the universal cousin the
ersal cousin the universal cousin the universal cousin the universal cousin the universa
n the universal cousin the universal cousin the universal cousin the universal cousin the
ersal cousin the universal cousin the universal cousin the universal cousin the universal cousin
universal cousin the universal cousin the universal cousin the universal cousin the universa
n the universal cousin the universal cousin the universal cousin the universal cousin the
ersal cousin the universal cousin the universal cousin the universal cousin the universal cousin
universal cousin the universal cousin the universal cousin the universal cousin the universa
n the universal cousin the universal cousin the universal cousin the universal cousin the
ersal cousin the universal cousin the universal cousin the universal cousin the universal cousin
universal cousin the universal cousin the universal cousin the universal cousin the universa
n the universal cousin the universal cousin the universal cousin the universal cousin the
ersal cousin the universal cousin the universal cousin the universal cousin the universal cousin
universal cousin the universal cousin the universal cousin the universal cousin the universa
n the universal cousin the universal cousin the universal cousin the universal cousin the
ersal cousin the universal cousin the universal cousin the universal cousin the universal cousin
universal cousin the universal cousin the universal cousin the universal cousin the universa
n the universal cousin the universal cousin the universal cousin the universal cousin the
ersal cousin the universal cousin the universal cousin the universal cousin the universal cousin
universal cousin the universal cousin the universal cousin the universal cousin the universa
n the universal cousin the universal cousin the universal cousin the universal cousin the
ersal cousin the universal cousin the universal cousin the universal cousin the universal cousin
universal cousin the universal cousin the universal cousin the universal cousin the universa
n the universal cousin the universal cousin the universal cousin the universal cousin the
ersal cousin the universal cousin the universal cousin the universal cousin the universal cousin
universal cousin the universal cousin the universal cousin the universal cousin the universa
n the universal cousin the universal cousin the universal cousin the universal cousin the
ersal cousin the universal cousin the universal cousin the universal cousin the universal cousin
universal cousin the universal cousin the universal cousin the universal cousin the universa
n the universal cousin the universal cousin the universal cousin the universal cousin the
ersal cousin the universal cousin the universal cousin the universal cousin the universal cousin
universal cousin the universal cousin the universal cousin the universal cousin the universa
n the universal cousin the universal cousin the universal cousin the universal cousin the
ersal cousin the universal cousin the universal cousin the universal cousin the universal cousin
universal cousin the universal cousin the universal cousin the universal cousin the universa
n the universal cousin the universal cousin the universal cousin the universal cousin the
ersal cousin the universal cousin the universal cousin the universal cousin the universal cousin
universal cousin the universal cousin the universal cousin the universal cousin the universa
n the universal cousin the universal cousin the universal cousin the universal cousin the
ersal cousin the universal cousin the universal cousin the universal cousin the universal cousin
universal cousin the universal cousin the universal cousin the universal cousin the universa
n the universal cousin the universal cousin the universal cousin the universal cousin the
ersal cousin the universal cousin the universal cousin the universal cousin the universal cousin
universal cousin the universal cousin the universal cousin the universal cousin the universa
n the universal cousin the universal cousin the universal cousin the universal cousin the
ersal cousin the universal cousin the universal cousin the universal cousin the universal cousin

He Is Risen

with His debilitating brain injury & His subsequently terminated employment.
He regards Us as a stranger deep

in the throngs of Union Square
where He hides from His family and nurses a burgeoning conviction —

The Universal Cousin!

strides out from The Total World System.
strides into The Apprehensible.

His face is like Our Own submerged in a distant
ocean where the warped light warps our features horribly back to us.

His separate extension cord plugs into the same original traumas
which discharge unto Him a variation of Our Own shock and awe.

He contorts His body and its attitudes in accordance
with the customs of a veiled city across the plains.

The fog, however briefly, lifts, and from Our perch
We note its landmarks: like inversions of Our Own:

The hospital **spitting**; The factory **splintering**
the sick into the parking lot; fine chairs of rich mahogany.

The differ-ence is We think Marx was pretty // much right. // The figures coming through the alleyway // resolve into actual people the moment We look at // Our bandage-spangled fists. Careful not to let the knife slip // from his hands. Yes the palatial Northeast // bowed to a fourth round of freezing rain. Still he leaned into this fire // of his own choosing, fate // being a series of gestures miming compulsion until the jig is up.

niversal cousin the universal cousin the universal cousin the universal cousin the universal
n the universal cousin the universal cousin the universal cousin the universal cousin the
rsal cousin the universal cousin the universal cousin the universal cousin the universal
n the universal cousin the universal cousin the universal cousin the universal cousin the
rsal cousin the universal cousin the universal cousin the universal cousin the universal
n the universal cousin the universal cousin the universal cousin the universal cousin the
rsal cousin the universal cousin the universal cousin the universal cousin the universal cousin the universal cousin
niversal cousin the universal cousin the universal cousin the universal cousin the universal
n the universal cousin the universal cousin the universal cousin the universal cousin the
rsal cousin the universal cousin the universal cousin the universal cousin the universal cousin the universal cousin
niversal cousin the universal cousin the universal cousin the universal cousin the universal
n the universal cousin the universal cousin the universal cousin the universal cousin the
rsal cousin the universal cousin the universal cousin the universal cousin the universal cousin the universal cousin
niversal cousin the universal cousin the universal cousin the universal cousin the universal
n the universal cousin the universal cousin the universal cousin the universal cousin the
rsal cousin the universal cousin the universal cousin the universal cousin the universal cousin the universal cousin
niversal cousin the universal cousin the universal cousin the universal cousin the universal
n the universal cousin the universal cousin the universal cousin the universal cousin the
rsal cousin the universal cousin the universal cousin the universal cousin the universal cousin the universal cousin
niversal cousin the universal cousin the universal cousin the universal cousin the universal
n the universal cousin the universal cousin the universal cousin the universal cousin the
rsal cousin the universal cousin the universal cousin the universal cousin the universal cousin the universal cousin
niversal cousin the universal cousin the universal cousin the universal cousin the universal
n the universal cousin the universal cousin the universal cousin the universal cousin the
rsal cousin the universal cousin the universal cousin the universal cousin the universal cousin the universal cousin
niversal cousin the universal cousin the universal cousin the universal cousin the universal
n the universal cousin the universal cousin the universal cousin the universal cousin the
rsal cousin the universal cousin the universal cousin the universal cousin the universal cousin the universal cousin
niversal cousin the universal cousin the universal cousin the universal cousin the universal
n the universal cousin the universal cousin the universal cousin the universal cousin the
rsal cousin the universal cousin the universal cousin the universal cousin the universal cousin the universal cousin
niversal cousin the universal cousin the universal cousin the universal cousin the universal
n the universal cousin the universal cousin the universal cousin the universal cousin the
rsal cousin the universal cousin the universal cousin the universal cousin the universal cousin the universal cousin
niversal cousin the universal cousin the universal cousin the universal cousin the universal
n the universal cousin the universal cousin the universal cousin the universal cousin the
rsal cousin the universal cousin the universal cousin the universal cousin the universal cousin the universal cousin
niversal cousin the universal cousin the universal cousin the universal cousin the universal
n the universal cousin the universal cousin the universal cousin the universal cousin the
rsal cousin the universal cousin the universal cousin the universal cousin the universal cousin the universal cousin
niversal cousin the universal cousin the universal cousin the universal cousin the universal
n the universal cousin the universal cousin the universal cousin the universal cousin the
rsal cousin the universal cousin the universal cousin the universal cousin the universal cousin the universal cousin
niversal cousin the universal cousin the universal cousin the universal cousin the universal
n the universal cousin the universal cousin the universal cousin the universal cousin the
rsal cousin the universal cousin the universal cousin the universal cousin the universal cousin the universal cousin
niversal cousin the universal cousin the universal cousin the universal cousin the universal
n the universal cousin the universal cousin the universal cousin the universal cousin the
rsal cousin the universal cousin the universal cousin the universal cousin the universal cousin the universal cousin

ACKNOWLEDGMENTS

To Francesca, without whom none of this works.

To Aaron and the rest of Broken Sleep Books, not only for their work on this volume, but for all the work they do as champions of a vital and vitally democratic vision of poetry.

To Molly, for reminding me that poetry is, yes, a social art form, and necessarily so in these times.

To Laurie, whose touch marks everything I write.

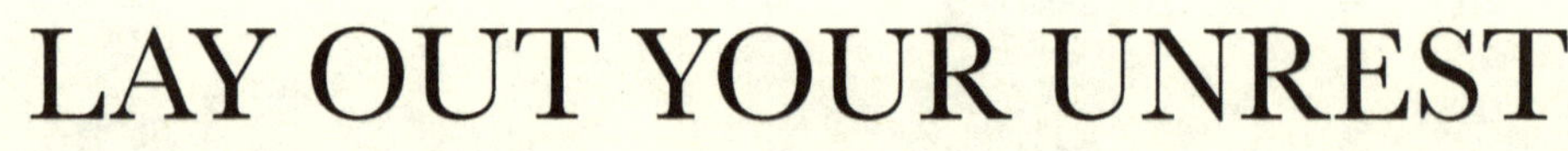
LAY OUT YOUR UNREST

www.ingramcontent.com/pod-product-compliance
Lightning Source LLC
LaVergne TN
LVHW051018080826
845145LV00009B/2691

* 9 7 8 1 9 1 7 6 1 7 6 1 1 *